Finding His Grace Everywhere

Lena Sain

WESTBOW
PRESS®
A DIVISION OF THOMAS NELSON
& ZONDERVAN

Scripture taken from the King James Version of the Bible.

WestBow Press books may be ordered through booksellers or by contacting:

WestBow Press
A Division of Thomas Nelson & Zondervan
1663 Liberty Drive
Bloomington, IN 47403
www.westbowpress.com
1 (866) 928-1240

ISBN: 978-1-5127-9655-1 (sc)
ISBN: 978-1-5127-9656-8 (e)

Library of Congress Control Number: 2017911277

Print information available on the last page.

WestBow Press rev. date: 08/30/2017

PART I

Introduction

Many people with whom I've shared my story have said that I should write a book, so I thought I should do it soon, since I am 80 years young! My only regret is that I might never hear from people who have been helped by the many blessings of my traumatic life.

MY SPIRITUAL GROWTH (or lack of it)

Easy to understand with my responsibilities with the 4 children growing up. And then, my "flesh" problem—I let too many things get in the way of what was most important. I had to be "Miss Polly perfect," SO no one would get wind of my real flaws. As I have said before, we moved so many times and I felt I must make curtains and decorate 47 houses over the years and I wanted to be involved in EVERYTHING.

I am afraid my spiritual growth was hindered a great deal, for which I am so very sorry. I missed a lot by being so BUSY! Besides, I don't really think that the condition of my salvation had become completely aware to me until very late. HE DIT IT ALL, FOLKS! He doesn't really NEED YOU; though you need Him. Give yourself to him--NO CONDITIONS, IF YOU PLEASE! AND YOUR FAMILY WILL LOVE YOU SO MUCH MORE !

DEDICATED TO MY MOTHER
Mary

About my Precious Mother whom I still love very dearly, even though she has gone to be with the Lord for many years. My mother lived her faith in spite of the many instances of abuse by her family and husband. Though she was only able to complete the third year of high school, she was a brilliant woman. She held several important jobs as an auditor in a local hotel and with another local business. She wrote plays for the Dr. Christian Radio Show, early in her life, winning prizes for the family. She was a Sunday School Teacher at her church, played the piano for services and was faithful in the outreach program there, as well as managing the grocery store. I really don't know how she did it, with 4 children and so much abuse.

However, I truly believe it was built into her heritage. My mother's family had many notable descendants. One was Chancellor at Oxford University in England, one invented the process of copper engraving; our family had two castles—one in England and one in Dublin, Ireland. She was also Creek and Cherokee Indian (part) and a relative of ours was once Mayor of a town in Tennessee. In fact, when the family first came to this country they bought about 2 or 3 states in the south, but were forced to sell some of them back (a good thing).

Her mother was a Nazarene Evangelist (she died when my mother was only ten and Mother was left with three brothers and her father (later a stepmother, whom she kept until the stepmother died). Her father was a policeman and worked also for a newspaper in Texas.

When my mother was ten, they moved to Georgia and had a very difficult life living with family. We were blessed to have my mother as a part of our life for several years.

I do not apologize for the many personal references in this, my TRUE story (1 Corinthians 15:10 "By the grace of God I am what I am, and His grace toward me was not in vain.") This book is mainly for readers undergoing similar situations, and do not know how to get the right kind of help. (Psalm 91:4

"For He shall cover you with His feathers and under His wings you shall take refuge.") In my book, you will see the many times My Lord has protected me with His wonderful HEDGES. It is important to this writer that you know what the most important HEDGE has been—that is, He buried my memories of the actual sexual experiences in my abuse, never to be a part of my life, ever again! I have a type of amnesia that has made a preposterous difference, for which I have been so blessed and HE did it! Praise the Lord for his care and deep love!

First, I am a blessed woman! I have the privilege of being a grandmother and great-grandmother of 43 wonderful children and my very own 5 children plus a better-than-average husband of 62 years, as well as an extended family unequalled by any others. Most of all, I am a born-again Christian; born to serve my Lord and Savior and I LOVE people! It has taken about 65 or 70 years to find the peace that was there for me all the time. He wanted to help me before then, but I refused His help so many times. (Psalm 91:2 "I will say of the Lord, He is my refuge and my fortress, my God, in Him will I trust.")

I should tell you about my wonderful extended family because there is no other family who has the compassion, love and care my family does. (1 Peter 4:8 "And above all things have fervent love for one another, for love will cover a multitude of sins".) My mother, as a single parent of 3 children, always had an extra job besides the grocery she successfully ran. My brother, even in high school, got a job at the local grocery store and gave everything he made to the family, mostly for food. We have been close and will be for as long as we live, and beyond! My sisters bless my life every day. I love them so!

My mother always wanted us to be close—AND WE ARE!

The following story will not be very nice, at first; in fact, yours may be even worse, I hope not. This story started at about 5 years of age when my father, who was a deranged person tried to blow up our house. My mother was a precious person who quickly sought help from her brother, my Uncle Jimmy.

We all moved in with Uncle Jimmy and Aunt Minnie, who already had 5 children of their own. We finally got things resolved and moved back home. Much precedes my story that is not pleasant, but the bad stuff began at age 11, when my father first began to molest and terrorize me. Having 2 younger sisters and a brother, I was given a bedroom of my own. This came in very handy for my father, who began to slip into my room after everyone else was asleep and begin his dastardly attacks.

Now at eleven I was responsible for my other siblings, doing the cooking, washing, cleaning, always trying to avoid my father (always on guard). Let me say at the very beginning that no one knew what was going on in the house, nobody at all except my father and myself. My siblings not only did not know that I had had my father's child, they did not even know that I had knowingly had sex with anyone. (Hard to believe, right?) That I know of, no one even knew I had a child by anyone until their siblings were grown and married, with children of their own.

We then moved to a nicer apartment where I once more became a "mom," cooking for the other 3 younger children, mostly French fries, hot dogs, etc., washing in a wringer washer with which I wasn't even familiar enough to know how to keep my arm out of it; as well as a pile of other duties as assigned. My mother was a hard worker, working at a hosiery mill, with long hard hours and though I didn't really appreciate my job, I did it and other things as well. My father began to abuse me; he would wake me up at night, unseen by the rest of the family; I just did not know how to handle the situation, there was no getting out of it. My mother, after her long days at work and at home slept very solidly. I was responsible for many other things such as helping a neighbor who was very sick and had small children, so I could not get help from her; I simply had no one to turn to and I did not yet know the Lord. Besides, my mother had a difficult marriage; in fact, she too was abused by her husband. When I was eleven, my father bought a grocery store and wanted ME to work there! Well, I knew how it was going to be, or I thought so. Was I ever wrong! He would take me off in the car and accelerate the car and threaten to run off a cliff if I didn't "cooperate." He took every opportunity to try getting me alone (when no customers were in the store) or in the storeroom, which I for the most part tried to avoid. One day he became very angry with my not "cooperating" and he kicked me very hard. At that time, the Colonial bread man happened to come in and catch him kicking me and we just about had to call the police. Many times, when my Dad got mad at mother and we would call the police, whom he knew, he would splash some liquor in his mouth and say something like, "Oh, we're just having a family argument" and because he knew the policemen—it was over. (Proverbs 29:20, "Do you see a man who is hasty in his words? There is more hope for a fool than for him.")

My life became a series of lies, which I hated. At the time, I was not saved and didn't know the consequences of lying, so I lied for convenience. I let everyone think that I had a pretty-much normal life. (Done that?) I loved school, it was my refuge at the time and I did well. Loved my teachers, loved books, loved my friends. I read every single chance I had and was a cheerleader, gymnast, and all-around likeable person—to everyone but myself. "Oh, what wicked lives we weave, when once we begin to deceive." I kept getting into trouble, as I didn't have enough to do and was put up in school two grades, which made me always the youngest in the class.

My BFF has always been there for me even though it was only recently I have shared my story with her; we have been friends for 69 years, loving and encouraging each other all along. (2 Corinthians 1:4 "Who comforts us in all our tribulation, that we may be able to comfort those who are in trouble, with the comfort with which we ourselves are comforted by God.") I thank the Lord for her friendship and I have learned so very much during that friendship; know she is my special angel and a wonderful sister in Christ; I know we will still be BFF when our life is over.

I never really had any boyfriends, no one ever knew that it was because my father ran them off as fast as they came. I once had a boy I really wanted to go out with, mainly because he had a plaid-top convertible, but my father met him at the car and told him it would be best if he never showed up there again! So much for boyfriends. I didn't want that embarrassment again, so I never showed any interest in anybody.

My Sunday School teacher, Mrs. Hall, led me to the Lord. She taught me so much more than the lessons, took a big interest in me and surely knew I was at least a very frightened young girl. I still love her very much, even though she has gone to be with the Lord long ago. (I hope if you have a need such as I had, you will seek out the help of someone just like Mrs. Hall, because you will surely need God's wisdom in your life!)

On one of the nights when my father was on one of his rampages, my precious Mother and my siblings, really needed help, as we had to escape very late (in our pajamas, yet). We hid in bushes and behind buildings; walking for miles, avoiding any cars that came by as we were headed for Grandmother's house. (Daddy had been giving Mother a very hard time and was drinking at that time and I had to literally "drag" her away from the house.) At that very moment, a nice man saw us running to the next bush and stopped to help us (my Protector, again). (Psalm 91:1 "He who dwells in the secret place of the Most High shall abide under the shadow of the Almighty.") He took us to my grandmother's house and she let us stay there overnight and it was soon after that when I had to tell my mother about becoming pregnant. She was devastated by the news, but could get me into a Florence Crittendon home. So, I left school, having only one more subject to finish high school at 16; I did return after the baby came and finished school.

I only told my mother and a friend of hers, who helped her to get help from a Doctor. I could NOT tell my mother who the father was at that time because I was afraid of what would happen when I had to go to have the baby, so I continued my charade then and when the baby was born, they put "Unknown" for the father's name—I said that I didn't know his name. I never even saw my baby because I knew I could not provide for her. I gave her up for adoption and went back to the home where they were so helpful. And. besides, I had heard so many things about children of incest not being healthy one way or another and I knew most certainly that I would not have the resources to be a good mother. The people at Florence Crittendon helped me to get a job in a nearby town and I was fortunate to get a room in a girls' home there, too. Was it all over; well I thought it was, but wouldn't you know, there He was again! Sitting outside my office with my mother in the car he said, "Get your things together, we're going home." All the way home, I prayed, "Oh Lord, you are not going to have me go through this again, are you?" And all the time I was thinking that I HAD to tell her; there must be an answer to this problem. There did come a convenient time; it was meant to be at that time. I had not been able to tell her before because of her problems with nerves, and I understood that very well. We were a dysfunctional family and I couldn't upset the apple cart, as it would hurt too many of my family. My sisters and brother had not a clue what was going on, did not even know I had a child.

So, first I ran away, just until I could get together a plan. My sweet grandmother let me hide in the upstairs bedroom, where all the grandchildren slept when they visited. I rode in to my job with my grandfather, very carefully hiding in the floorboard of the car as we went past our grocery store on the way downtown. He worked at a local Cola company as a carpenter, so it wasn't too far out of the way. (He was such a funny driver; sitting very erectly in his seat.) I really came to appreciate him as we became acquainted. I found out that he had once been a part of a country band, playing the mandolin very well, on the weekends. They were very good to me, letting me stay until I got a room with a very nice lady over in a nice neighborhood. That did not last long, though because one day I came out the door at work; my father had found me, and even though I refused, he said he would follow me home and honk the horn outside my new home until I came out. In the meantime, he boarded up the windows and doors in the back of the house so I couldn't get in any way but the front door, in case I tried to come and get my clothes and he could watch for me from the store.

That was it! I got my mother aside and told her the whole story and we went straight to the Doctor's office for a consultation and then to the Judge's office, where he put out a warrant for my father's arrest and sent him to a mental institution where they tried to break him down but couldn't.

For a while, he was no longer a threat to me or my family and though it was hard for us to run the grocery store, we continued to do it together, as I had gotten my driver's license early and was able to pick up the stock for the store. Mother made it work, even though she almost lost her mind about this. In the meantime, my uncle (my father's brother) began to make threatening phone calls. There was a big family rift because of me and mother having caused Daddy to be put away. And, one day we found out that my uncle came to visit father and took him away and he never came back. No one ever looked for him.

We found out that he had gotten a job at a grocery store in another town nearby and even had remarried and had a family!

I kept working at my job and at the grocery store, scared to death he would come back. (Psalm 139:13:1 "For thou hast possessed my reins, thou hast covered me in my mother's womb. 14: I will praise thee; for I am fearfully and wonderfully made, marvelous are thy works; and that my soul knoweth right well.")

Our Marriage

*B*ut in the meantime, the Lord had sent an angel into my life and I fell deeply in love. After telling him about my situation he still wanted to marry me and we became engaged on February 10th and got married on March 26, 1955. (because he had orders to go to California to Chinese language school, of all things.) And they said it wouldn't last, but here we are 62 years later and he is just as kind and tender as he was the first time I met him. (There were some bad years, which did scar things rather badly, but His HEDGE was there. Thank you, dear God!) We met on a blind date at church. I had gotten saved prior to that and I thought because we needed each other it would be alright if he just got saved later. Well, that was a big mistake, I was so much in love that I just overlooked that as being one of God's greatest teachings--a great big mistake for anyone to make, by the way, and we paid dearly for that one!

So, there we were, a couple who knew little about marriage (of the right kind) and it was a miserable 10 years. We really had it rough. The chaplain who counseled with us told us to go away and never let my family know where we were living. But he just didn't know how much we loved my family and we just couldn't comply with his wishes.

My mother had sold the store by that time and there was no reason for them to stay there, so we packed up (just like the Clampett's) all squeezed into our one car and left for the big old world out there with that GREAT BIG OLD HEDGE securely around us. The neighbors told us that my father had found our house and came, looking for us 30 minutes later.

Praise the Lord! We rented apartments for the two families because mainly, it was a condemned house, in fact the only one that when the hurricane came through it missed us! There was no place to live back then.

Mother got a job with a jewelry store in town, my husband went off to his Army job and the kids went to the local schools. By that time, I became pregnant, so my dog and I stayed home for a little while.

We were all so thankful to be safe and have a home near each other, things went rather well for a while. My husband played French horn and the bugle and our food budget was helped a good bit by our being able to go to a lot of local food gatherings as my husband's band played in many parades for the Army. (I DID REMEMBER ONE TIME LAUGHING BECAUSE WE HAD ONLY ONE PRENATAL VITAMIN ON OUR PLATES FOR DINNER!)

Later, my family went back home because mother's job played out. And when I went to work for Civil Service, the family wanted to get back to their friends, so they moved back home and since my father had remarried, they didn't fear his being in the picture any more. However, not the same with me, unfortunately, as I had a great deal of flashbacks and didn't quite have their faith. (2 Corinthians 12:9 "And He said to me, 'My Grace is sufficient for you, for my strength is made perfect in weakness.' "I therefore, most gladly will rather boast of my infirmities that the power of Christ may rest upon me.") Thank goodness, I didn't have to go down the same streets and see the same sights that had terrorized me as before.

Do you ever have flashbacks? I really hated those and the nightmares. Over the years, the Lord has helped me both to forgive my father and to visit him before he died. When you forgive something like this you must forget that you were wronged and never forget who showed you the way to forgiveness. Thank you, LORD! (2 Phillippians 3:13-14, "But one thing I do, forgetting those things which are behind and looking forward to those things which are ahead; 14. I press forward for the prize of the upward call of God in Christ Jesus....")

Our Children

Now, here's the very best part of our life—God has blessed us with five (5) wonderful children. We had four of our own and one child by my father, and we have loved every single one of them and are so very proud of each of them—still. Each has had an interesting life, and though we feel we may have failed them in many ways (we had to "grow up" **with** them). Some mistakes were made (mostly on our parts and through wrong choices.) Well, let's just see how it all came out....

Patricia, our "eldest," as she had and still does, call her name for herself came to us for the first time at 53. We received a letter, a real surprise, from the State, telling us that she was my daughter, and living nearby; and she would like to establish a relationship with me. Would we consider a visit or letter from her?

From then on, there was an outpouring of love involving our whole family, except my father who was then deceased. We grew to know and love her very much and found out we had so much in common, including our love for the Lord to start with. We met all her family, including her husband, who subsequently died, and loved every one of them. Her adopted parents had passed away before this time, but we got a wonderful book that Patricia had put together about her life in that family—all of them. Already you can see God's hand in this as we all needed each other to love. (1 Peter 4:8 "And above all things have fervent love for one another; 'love will cover a multitude of sins.'")

You do not have to become ashamed because of your family's choices, become a druggie or consort with the wrong crowd and your family can be all you want—really want—it to be. It's up to you, dear friend.

Patricia had one daughter, Anna, who had helped her mother to find me, and she had a grandson, Brad, whom she raised and Timothy (Anna's husband,) who is just grand! God IS SO GOOD! Very soon after, little Emily came along—a beautiful baby! She is now a lovely young lady, too!

Our first child was born on July 3, 1956. We sure learned a lot because God knew we didn't know A THING about babies. But, Miss Lynn showed us all we needed to know and we loved her dearly. She woke me up one morning to tell me that she had an angel on her bed during the night and, since then, she has always served the Lord faithfully, using her tremendous voice and her teaching skills for 25+years. Her whole family practically are in the Lord's service in some way or another. She has a fine Christian husband named Harold, who is a faithful deacon; and four wonderful and beautiful girls and nine beautiful grandchildren. (I did finally learn that you didn't need to sterilize the bottle brushes—didn't take long, either.)

Later, we had wonderful picnics at the zoo, swimming and camping.

I sewed a lot then, making all the girls' dresses for the Inspirations, for whom she and her sister, Joyce sang. (I even thought I was smart enough to make Lynn's wedding dress, just like she wanted; and all the attendants' dresses at the wedding, too. We communicated by phone and put the wedding together from the farm, travelling to the Bible College where Harold and Lynn were married!) I could praise them forever for their love and care of their children AND their parents, but then, I'm prejudiced!

Joyce has always been a JOY indeed; although we didn't always agree about things. This made her very sad. She was brilliant, having taken college studies while in high school. Born August 18, 1957, she was saved at 14 and has taken care of her entire family of two boys, a daughter-in-law and two precious girls, her grandchildren. It breaks my heart to see her struggle as she has taken on the whole load for herself. She really hasn't had much of a chance at a life of her own, much of which was my fault. In my heart, I knew I hurt her badly, but I never could shut my big mouth. By the way, I was born Irish and Creek Indian; thus, my "open-mouth-insert-foot" personality. I have since asked her to forgive me and I am sure she has. God has been so good to me! Something good IS going to happen! Joyce was a medical and legal transcriptionist who worked much too much, giving her a few health issues. Bless her, Lord. She has a beautiful voice and sang with the Inspirations at church, as well as in a pizza parlor. She also wrote and recorded a beautiful song for her husband, which I still listen to, even though he's gone. She is a wonderful grandmother and her two boys and daughter-in-law as well as the two grandchildren all live together, farthest away from us of all the children. We miss a lot! (Author's note: She's coming to see US in May—Lord willing!)

Earl has always been a loving, caring boy and young man. Born March 24, 1960, he was always a bit shy and at 12 he began to develop signs of some mental problems. He made good grades and though he didn't have many friends, all who knew him really loved him. He was named after his grandfather and an uncle – He was in Cub Scouts and played remedial softball. He loved the outdoors and once thought about becoming a Forest Ranger.

He was saved at 11 or 12 and was the most caring son, brother and husband and father in the world. Very much loved by all the family. After his marriage, he and his wife, Terry, had two wonderful children and now, two perfect grandchildren—Amy and Bob—Kathleen (married to Danny) and Dustin, who is 31 and staying single.

Earl worked for 15 years with the same lumber company, winning awards and prizes all the while, but landed in the middle of a great disagreement which ended his job there. Every job he performed in an excellent manner, receiving accolades attesting to the same.

However, we soon learned he had five mental illnesses--the greatest one being Alzheimer's disease at 56; he also had schizophrenia, bipolar disease, panic disorder and paranoia. We have been his caregivers while his family worked for about 10 years, bonding in as many ways as possible. We are now 80 and 81 and caring and bonding with him has given us a whole new attitude about mental illness. He has a psychiatrist and takes many medicines. He also has counselors and a neurologist. The main thing we have noticed during our time as his caregivers is that he is still as sweet as he always was and except for the fact that there is not much talking, or social interchange, as a rule.

He helped in the restoration of our 100-year-old home, which was right next door to him, and he did a marvelous job. He appreciates and thanks us always and still helps us out and reads his Bible. He now attends church with us and we still pray that miracles continue to happen again. God takes such good care of him and us! He spent some time in a mental hospital for a good while, as they adjusted the many medications. We are so proud of him. He still sees his psychiatrist and other counselors, now. He delights in seeing his grandchildren!

(There was a missed-abortion in between Earl and our last child, Kayce. I had contracted measles.)

Now you couldn't help but like Kayce. Not only was she the youngest, but because of her health issues, she had her mother's ear and heart. I have already said that I loved them equally; however, Kayce had so many health issues and my goal was to help her to live with those. At one month old, she had to wear braces; later corrective shoes. She was required to wear a full-body brace (Milwaukee) during her teen-age years, due to Scoliosis. She was unfortunately divorced and remarried 3 times and when she died at 46, from cancer (she had AML), she and her husband, John had six children, college-aged and under high school age.

One of them, Candy, had a very traumatic time during her pre-teens, being molested by her choir director at church. We were aware of it and tried to help, to no avail, as the pastor did not believe her. And, her mother was in a divorce at the time, so no help was given to either of them. She is such a precious child, and it is our hope her faith will be restored soon. We love her so much. She stayed with us in her earlier years while her mother went through the divorce and rehab for an addiction to cigarettes and Dr. Pepper. Kayce was always very helpful to others at rehab. She had such a rough time with her breast cancer, then AML and all her trips to a cancer treatment in Ohio for treatments, most of which she drove to and from herself.

At her funeral, her stepson, James, wrote and read a beautiful poem about her life and

I have taken the privilege of including it, with his permission by the way, it so that you may appreciate her life as we have. She gladly gave her testimony to many radio stations in Toledo, at other functions and her church. She was an accomplished artist and made many sets for her church.

Your Song

The night has come once again and your memory comes over me.

In the wind, I feel your soul.

You finished the race; you made it your goal.

You touched our lives and changed them forever.

You showed us what it meant to fight, through this endeavor.

You were as kind and gentle as you could be.

The love for us all, you showed to me.

Your smile, your laugh we'll never forget.

The time we had with you we'll never regret.

It seems too soon that you're gone away,

But we'll all feel your embrace again someday.

You were always there to help when you were needed and always picked us back up when we felt defeated.

Your life was a song of grace,

To live for someone else, that's all you ever did.

You were there since we were kids.

As the angels in the heavenly realms sing, we know you're with Him, now and forever

Our Father and King.

By James Creamer (Kayce's stepson)

Not to worry:
God is in control; read the following pages in Part II and learn how God handles his adventurous one, Ollie, as Fran nervously shakes her head, and Chunky barks— LOUDLY! He was a faithful friend for the past 19 years!
AND NOW...HERE'S "THE REST OF THE STORY...."

PART II

Chapter 1

FAMILY MOVED TO N.C., PROVIDENTIALLY

*Y*es, we did it ALL in our little green Ford! When the Chaplain advised us to go away and not let even our family know where we were; that burned; this family has always been very close and we love them so much.

However, we were afraid our father would find us and do great harm to us, so we hurried as fast as our well-packed Ford would let us, with a mattress on top, secured by an old rope we had located in the garage. Well, it was so far to our new home that we had to make a bathroom/food stop somewhere up there, and my six-foot-two mother had to crawl out the back window to get out of the car and SHE DID IT! She really did it! (Wish I'd been gutsy enough to do that!) She made it back into the windows, also, and off we went! Once we got there, we rented a big old farm house with two apartments and a good old farmer and his sweet wife! (Thanks again, Lord!)

When we called back home, our neighbor told us that our father had found the house where we had lived 30 minutes after we had left town. (We knew that his brother had come to visit him at the Mental Center where the Judge had sent him and just took him away and the courts never tried to find him!) We understood much later that he had even remarried and had a family.

Chapter 2

HOUSE AFIRE ON RAY AVENUE (our New house)

Being in the Army, Ollie was sent to an Army base in N.C., where there were pitifully-few-to-none houses available. We wanted to be together, right? So, my husband rented the room in the back at the kind farmer's home and we shared a bath and had an oil cook stove in the kitchen. (We had to go out in the chicken yard to get fresh oil--a hoot!)

Anyway, one day I was preparing to cook dinner and we smelled smoke coming around the side of the house (we were on the front porch, rocking.) Ollie went to investigate and he said, "Get me an axe! The kitchen is on fire" I had forgotten to turn the kerosene container upright when I brought the oil in from the chicken yard! Well, it was just like the Keystone Cops and Mighty Ollie went to work putting the fire out, in the kitchen wall!

Wait until you hear MY part in this little adventure! In addition to messing up the placement of the oil, we had long Priscilla curtains (white ones, at that); guess who was elected to wash and IRON EVERY SINGLE ONE OF THEM and REDO THE BEDCLOTHES, AS WELL? Thank you Lord for an understanding husband AND LANDLORD! I was happy to do that, so we could have the room and be together. That enabled us to withstand the unbearable pain at having to wash the bathtub out each time we wanted to get a bath, due to the fact that the farmer chose to spit in the tub quite frequently! (After all, it WAS HIS TUB!) But, being newlyweds and having had to stay with in-laws for 3 weeks--no problem! We were even thankful that Hurricane Hazel left most of the house intact. We were served our first meal in the new palace the night before (quite a spread.) Thank you, God, for your wonderful HEDGE!

Chapter 3

MOVING AGAIN TO ANOTHER APARTMENT

We really did love the farmer and his wife (and all the food) but after our main man fell through the front porch one morning on the way to work and we had set the house on fire AND I had to iron all those curtains, the "team" began to look for another place for all of us to live. We moved down the street, closer to the jewelry store my mother then worked for and OF COURSE, we were still greenhorns again! We had a coal stove to heat the house with and when mother got us some coal, she forgot to tell us how much to put in it, so with our usual thinking (more is better, isn't it?) we nearly burned THAT place down. In fact, the neighbors down in the first-floor apartment started moving their things out into the street. I THINK WE MAY HAVE PUT JUST A TAD TOO MUCH COAL INTO THAT STOVE! OOPS! How that paint did bubble! And, of course our reliable in-house handyman was not home; he was at work! Well, that stove really got hot then, so we just managed the best we could, and got outside for a while. Oh yes, we did know better than to ADD more COAL!

Believe me! By then I was sure hoping that God had not forgotten where we had moved, because WE DESPERATELY NEEDED ANOTHER HEDGE, THANKS AGAIN, GOD!

Chapter 4

A CIVIL SERVICE JOB FINALLY CAME THROUGH FOR MOM! AS OLLIE GOT IN THE BAND!

Ollie finally got a band job (he played the French horn and bugle).

Later, he got into Air Traffic Controller School, and what do you know—a baby—little Lynn, appeared back home!

We were so fortunate to have a dear friend, a lady named Corrine (her mother was a cook at The Rockefellar place In Southern Pines). Corrinne literally saved our lives when Ollie was in that school. She brought us plenty of food and cooked it for us after she got off work! We had no kerosene to heat with and she brought us some of that, too. My husband got passed up for E-4, even though he was attending ATC school and making passing grades. We didn't even make enough to live on, even with just one baby and my having recently gotten a GS-3 job! Of course, we never forgot those dear friends, who had been there for us – they were SPECIAL ANGELS! –HEDGES!

Chapter 5

MIGHTY OLLIE TO THE RESCUE! AGAIN! BLESS HIS HEART!

Speaking of hard times, we decided to take a chance on an old car we had traded our one air conditioner on and take a fun trip to the beach, where Ollie incidentally saw a family in trouble with the under tow and he, of course, dashed to the rescue.

The people (3 of them) were so nice and corresponded with us for quite a while. A blessing for the family and us.

In the meantime, we kept going in our "New" old car until we had more company. (We had a crank-out windshield and were attacked by a swarm of angry bees!)

(Could not get the crank to turn as fast as the bees!) Ollie could hardly get the car stopped, with those good old mechanical brakes; that wasn't good enough for me and my new baby, so I figured out how to open that old door and me and my little one ditched that antiquity! No one got hurt, naturally, with her blankets securely around her and all that sand around, too. Well, it was right about then that we had decided we were NOT going to make it in the Army, no matter how much FUN we were having!

We stayed until Ollie had finished school and we had another baby, another beautiful girl, and just before Ollie's discharge our son was born!

We had to get a hardship discharge, after all. But, Ollie got a jazzy job at a miniature golf course. That was a big challenge—a miniature golf course with all those kids, teenagers, plus he didn't have too much "kid savvy".

Chapter 6

<u>THEN OLLIE WENT TO OKLAHOMA CITY TO GO TO AIR TRAFFIC CONTROL
SCHOOL YOU KNOW:</u>

The place where they teach guys and gals to either go nuts, get a divorce, or become an alcoholic—by the way, we did none of the above—he passed so beautifully! GOD'S HEDGES ONCE MORE!

He was first assigned to Columbus, Ohio and then, before the paint got dry, to Burlington, Vermont, where we found a real dream house to live in and though we still did not make much money, we managed. The house was 90 years old and had been beautifully renovated and when we opened our bedroom curtains, there was beautiful Mount Mansfield to greet us! Thank you, God, so very much!

However, there was one big problem—we lived in between two Mountains and I became terrified again, SOMEONE was trying to break into our upstairs bedroom—NO DOUBT! I first tried to find neighbors by phone to get help (we were out in the "boonies") NO ONE ANSWERED—NOT ONE! So, I did the next best thing—I called dear Ollie at the airport— which was a no-no, and told him about the situation and he luckily had back-up at work, so he came home to find me TERRIFIED, with the shutters upstairs still banging relentlessly and me locked in the bathroom (for protection). He naturally went up to investigate and heard FIREWORKS coming from Colchester, nearby. It was the Fourth of July and they had echoed between the mountains!

Well, that wasn't quite as bad as the mouse who entered the house, causing me to call the landlord frantically (REALLY a greenhorn! AGAIN). He told me it was just a "little" field mouse, (Which didn't help a bit!) THANK GOD for His protection, AGAIN!

Chapter 7

WE ARE GOING SOUTH AGAIN, AND LOVING IT!

*D*ue to some personal problems, we were forced to move in with my mother, for a little while. When my husband moved down from Vermont, he got a job at Ft. Rucker, Al., where he helped train U. S. Army helicopter pilots. This began a whole new lifestyle for us. I got a job with the Army (an aviation technical magazine,) doing some typing and editorial work. Also, my department proofed the magazine galleys each month, which was, for me, a very exciting trip, in a rickety old UH-19 helicopter!

God provided a wonderful home in Al. And WOW! Things really popped then! We did discover, however, that Joyce, our second child, had what the doctors thought was osteomyelitis OR rheumatic fever (they weren't sure which). Since we had to carry her up and down the stairs and I was also pregnant with our youngest child, we moved to a town nearby where her doctors and hospital were. After many hospitalizations and questions, she did have osteomyelitis and eventually recovered. In the meantime, we settled in our new house, and with our new (and last) baby, Kayce, and with God's help got Joyce well and mommy, too, so all is well! House, too! Baby, too, we thought.

A friend in Air Traffic Control told Ollie about a revival at his church and that he wanted Ollie to go with him. He went, and Praise the Lord, he got saved that night and he took me to that revival the very next night and I rededicated my life to the Lord! That was the beginning of the rest of our wonderful life! We began to attend church regularly and participate as well as we could, teaching and attending as many extra classes as we could. We really loved those people and they loved all of us, especially our Kayce, who was required to wear a pillow splint to straighten a deformity in her hip. Then the Doctor put her in braces on her feet and eventually shoes with braces. She kept smiling and going, though, and we were so blessed. GOD'S HEDGES AGAIN!

Chapter 8

WE ARE GOING TO PUERTO RICO (ACTUALLY OUT OF THE COUNTRY) WOW!

*M*any interesting things happened to us there, but we enjoyed the people, learned some Spanish, ate platanos, and went to a Nazarene church; and best of all, met some great people AND animals.

The most interesting place we lived in was in Rio Piedras, where we rented the home of a CIA man and his wife, a Spiritualist White Queen. They had left some furniture in the house and some dust in the corners (we assumed!); otherwise, it was a beautiful house with a balcony, wrought iron doors, and a patio. We did find a few things we should replace, such as the preserved chicken-heads, the dust in the corners and fruit stains on the back-bedroom floor—we did use the curved glassed-in cupboard (the one which had held the chicken-heads) for other things. I was told by Edil (who was married to my friend, Lilli, a proper English woman) that I'd "best just leave the dust in the corners;" "because that would keep those evil spirits away from our home!" Oh yes, and a beautiful bidet in the master bathroom! I had to watch some of the children closely; they thought it was a water Fountain!

We really enjoyed getting to know our neighbors across the street, (Paul, Celeste and Judith). They were originally from New Jersey and Paul worked on a lot of fancy government clocks. They had a flat-topped house, as did most people, and the most unusual situation—two goats, very good-looking AND smart. At night, they climbed up the ladder to the top of the house and even had beds of some kind there, too! Every day Paul would take them to the local "colmado" (grocery store) and they knew where to find their favorite candies (wrapped caramels); wasn't hard to get the paper off, either! Then they strolled back home, blissfully enjoying their trip.

One week, Paul and Celeste and Judith wanted us to join them at the beach. They took Benny and Cecil and all of us, right out in the ocean—almost. Benny and Cecil's favorite outing! The interesting thing about our children was that they wouldn't ride with us in our great big Volkswagen bus; they insisted on riding in the car with the goats. Judith had on a big straw hat which the goats chewed as we went. We had a good laugh about that and Benny and Cecil were very obedient pets—how much fun we did have!

ONE other little item of interest: In September, I went shopping for a new dress for a birthday celebration at the Navy Club on the island. I never noticed my lights being gone, but every kid on the Island told us about that! Thanks to a smart husband, we "BOUGHT OUR OWN LIGHTS BACK JUST IN TIME FOR DINNER;" had a wonderful time, anyway! THANK GOD FOR THOSE HEDGES!

Mama and Papa visited in December, as did some of our associational missionaries from the States and we had to "Trivago" to acquire additional room for everyone. But, our friends were helpful and we almost had a pretty good visit with almost everybody! There was a little snag, though. We took Mom and Pop down to the dock where their "ship" The Dora Kay was, and we were ALL dismayed at the smallness of our "ship." Well, Mama and Papa wanted very much to visit St. Thomas, one of the destinations, so they honored their commitments to go UNTIL—Papa became very ill first and then Mama. (A major case of sea-sickness!) To make a long story short—GUESS WHO was sitting on our front steps when we got home from church—you can guess, of course—a very greenish-looking couple of greenhorns, who had taken a plane back from the island they so much wanted to see!

After a short nap, they felt like visiting our guests--a very nice couple of men from the church, and we all enjoyed our version of Island cuisine.

Chapter 9

AFTER ALL THAT FUN IN PUERTO RICO, WE WERE TRANSFERRED TO MIAMI, FLORIDA! (BUT WE DIDN'T STAY LONG!)

My husband accepted a nice transfer, courtesy of a long-time friend and we went to Miami, high and dry, (and, that was one winner of a home!), especially the sea grape tree in the pool which the kids loved to swing on into the pool—beautifully landscaped, with a circle driveway, excellent schools in a great neighborhood. We really loved the house, neighbors, and pool, but it was time to go again which was okay for the money, which we weren't so used to. However, there was just one little hitch! We had entrusted the management to a fellow employee who had sold it (we thought) to a customer who signed a bogus contract (unbeknownst to the former owners—US) and there we were on our way to Phoenix to our new job with an OLD HOUSE still officially UNSOLD! AND THE REST OF THAT STORY IS...2 MORE YEARS OF RENTING A HOUSE TO LIVE IN WHILE WERE THERE AND PAYING THE WHOLE MORTGAGE IN MIAMI! If that wasn't our bad luck, AGAIN, I don't know what would be. We heard on the news, though, that Hurricane Andrew in 1992 completely wiped out our entire community; even the street signs, after we were gone, so I guess that was sort of "good luck, for us," after all.

Chapter 10

OUR LAST STOP WAS PHOENIX, WITH NEW CAREERS ALL AROUND, ADVENTURE AND TWO TIRED OLD GEEZERS!

*A*s I have said in the last chapter we were now in Phoenix, in a rental home, with an UNSOLD HOME, and, oh, well we just went to work at our new jobs, smiling. Fran didn't keep that smile very long. On her very first day at the N.L.R.B. in town she was caught up in one of Arizona's famous FLASH FLOODS. No way out, short of climbing a few trees and swinging. Nothing to do but wait for help.

So, I did just that and when I finally got to the new job right down on Central Avenue, I hastily apologized for my lateness and got the job anyway—they must have been desperate for help. My job with the Board was very interesting, with several well-informed lawyers—WELL INFORMED—with a great display of management; which gave me a chance to think about my choices.

The first or second day a bunch of lumber-yard workers hit the third floor and my choice was made. The first at my desk was a guy with a rough-and-tumbled look, sans shoes, who went straight to *MOI* desk, which was right in front of the door and announced, "There's gonna' be some blood spilled down at that yard, today." He was evidently talking about the lumber yard where he worked. At that point, I excused myself to go to the ladies' room, and let someone bigger than myself speak with him. I grabbed my wig out of the ladies' room—and headed for my new rental home! That husband of mine; it's all his fault, coming way out here for an old Promotion! Then I said to myself, "I think I'll check out the medical profession in Phoenix, just to see if I can qualify." After a two-week notice, during which I reluctantly typed and edited my last brief, I went over, took a test at a local medical facility, did fairly well, enrolled in Good Sam Hospital's branch of Maricopa Technical College and—WALLA—I became the latest member of the staff the at the Health Plan!

Look at me, Mom, "I'm a medical transcriptionist and I can spell some big words like 'Cardiologist.'" From that day on, after taking tests each night, my life changed drastically; learning things like "hernias" and "hemorrhoids." Worked for some fantastic doctors and nurses, and just retired, after thirty-three years! Worked for Dr. Jack Hughston, AKA "DR.

KNEE"—and that's where I had my implanted knees, put in by one of his top assistants 25 years ago—Fine and Dandy (my new Titanium knees) are still showing very little wear today!

My brilliant husband had to retire from Air Traffic Control, giving up also his private pilot's license, after 25 years of government service, because of a condition known as "Ophthalmic Migraines." He lost some of his sight. He was offered desk jobs in Los Angeles, CA and Washington, D.C. (bad for a house full of teenagers and college students.) So, after attending college and receiving an AA degree (sume cum laude) we began to research jobs in the midwestern states.

Chapter 11

I LIKED PINK HOUSES ANYWAY (AND THE PINK 5-HOLER OUTHOUSE, TOO!)

*I*t was tough, even with all of us pitching in, to get past the graduations in Phoenix, packing, and cleaning, but we worked like a bunch of "mighty mice" and were on the road to another adventure after we dropped off our second daughter, Joyce, at a local college, where she was to attend. And, not the least—loading up our moving truck, snowmobile, second car (Earl's) and another truck, plus the cats and dogs (bless their hearts). We really had to hustle to get ready to go. However, with mop and broom in hand and me looking like a witch, we went! Our first hitch came very close to home, at the motel where we had decided to stay in that night, when we met the world's grumpiest old man-- a hotel clerk with maybe just a wee bit too much to drink. My husband would usually take care of such a situation but was tied up with the moving truck and a couple of animals, so there I was 'in charge!" We really looked pitiful after a day of very hard work and the man was just in no mood to fool with such a bunch of hillbillies and didn't hesitate to tell us he "hoped we would go somewhere else!" I didn't tell Ollie all he'd said, I just said, "We'd better go—looks like this one is all filled up." (I sure didn't want any blood spilled down there!)

However, when we came to a unique street arrangement in town, there were all kinds of businesses on both sides, north and south; we became everlastingly separated from the two guys, who thought I was just going too fast and tried to catch up with me; (they drove all the way to the farm) AND AT THAT POINT—I RAN OUT OF GAS! NO MEN! NO MONEY! NO GAS! NO WHERE TO CALL!

However, my sweet Ollie got hold of a local sheriff, who then looked for me until he found me and my daughter, Kayce. Both of us were near tears and mad as two wet hens; we had sincerely planned to hang both of our men from the second floor of the barn or somewhere dark and danky. Such humility! Well, the tears were dry when we finally got some gas, money and a Diet Coke and we saw the farm. By that time, it was morning and a beautiful sight. Wow! were we surprised! The rolling hills (210 acres), the gorgeous barn, which once was used by the owners for good old fashioned barn dances, even the mink farm, which was protected from air traffic coming over, not to mention the 5-holer pink outhouse with **"Instructions for What to do in case of a Tornado"** placed on the wall."

The house, just an average, everyday pink house contained 3 big bedrooms an indoor bathroom, a large farmhouse kitchen, and a very necessary mud room. We wanted to see the big town, meet its Mayor and check out Ollie's work place. An old-fashioned town, with Dot's Café, which had "Oofta" cups (to see who paid for the coffee!) I really loved that place. We spent a little over an hour just riding in the truck, up and down those beautiful hills, which we had rented out. Then we settled down to "moving in." Lots to do, with checking out the Homemakers' Club, the Mayor's wife and children, and of course our neighbors, who were our friends for years. She was my Irish friend and her husband was a pilot in Alaska and presently a horse owner and farmer. We had a great time with all the local people, while in that little town; but it became a great burden for my Ollie and we began to regret the move and started trying to work out a sale. We had purchased some prize sheep (Hampshire) and a very ornery stud. He was a beautiful horse and so very fast! But he had a lousy temperament (he chewed the sheep's wool off and was very unmanageable for any of us—some dilemma for greenhorns like us!). Albert, our friend and neighbor came over and gave us lessons in horse management—He had many horses. Holding the stud's bridle, he gave him a huge uppercut with his fist and from then on, he never acted up again (with Albert)!

We had decided to sell the farmhouse and go home to the house my mother had lived in most of her life, which was now FOR SALE! Wouldn't you know there was a hidden clause that said that we couldn't sell the farm property without the farmer's permission! Naturally, he was giving us fits, turning down everyone who wanted to buy the house! Well, my Ollie had become friends with a lot of local people and it seems the local banker decided to get into the mix and helped us to accomplish this feat! Praise the Lord – HEDGES!

In the meantime, I had a job to do. Our daughter, Lynn, and her fiancé, Harold finished college in Springfield, MO. And we had a wedding to finish! I had finished Lynn's wedding dress, but still lacked the attendants' dresses, these were from all over the U.S. I finally got this done just in time for the wedding, including the Flower Girl's dress; we rounded up all the people—including both grandparents and had a beautiful wedding in Missouri!

Then we took almost all the family back home with us to the farm. They loved it, too, but we were very much inclined to sell it. After securing a buyer, we had an auction! Sold Mindy, Molly, Puff and Stuff, Piff, Poff, and Poof for exactly what we had paid for them. Sold the ornery horse for "$25.00 and threw in the bridle!" We prepared for our move back down South. The family home (150 years old) was for sale and we bought it! My mother had lived there as a child, so she checked it out for us and off we went. (A lot of "winter mishaps" happened to confirm our decision to go "home.") "Home" was a beautiful thought. Although we knew it would be a lot of "sweat and tears," we eagerly looked forward to seeing and knowing the "homeplace".

Chapter 12

HOME SWEET HOME! WAVERLY HALL, GEORGIA

The last memories of my grandparents' home were tins of BUTTONS! When we would go to visit, I remembered my Mama Minnie would gently place me in the parlor on the sofa with a tin of buttons. (Then children were not allowed to run or jump around in certain rooms!) So, I had a wonderful time trying to figure out who had owned these beautiful buttons. I had quite an imagination and entertained myself for hours imagining who they were, where they lived and what they were!

We began to renovate the house by locating contractors for different problems of the house and what a hassle that was. We would get an agreement for some contractor and he would immediately disappear! And then there was Golden. Golden Barber was an elderly man who had worked for my grandfather and he had a dog named "Spoat" (short for Sport) who came with him one day to work; Golden told me that he had worked for "Mr. Teenor" and he wanted to work for us now. He forgot one major thing: He was blind as he could be; I didn't find that out until I was up on the ladder scraping the old buttermilk paint off the house; he had the TORCH! So, we had to give him another job immediately or burn the house down! HEDGES!

At any rate, we finished the house and had a wonderful Tour of Homes, sponsored by one of the teachers at the high school (the former owners) and showed off royally, (with a little help from a lot of friends and neighbors). On the inside of the house, we had a little trouble getting the wallpaper to stay on the wall! Every morning, after working hard and late, we would come down the stairs and it was curled up on the floor. There was much speculation about "Ghosts" which we were beginning to believe, especially after we had to hire professionals and the very same thing happened with them. We did not want to deal with it so we found a solution; we went downtown to the lumber people and bought paneling; came home and put it up "wrong-side" out and the wallpaper stayed until they demolished the house!

After the Tour, I got involved with "Up with People," a fine organization with some great young talent and I was the coordinator, getting them places to stay and making plans for appearances. We had the concert in our gym and it was outstanding! There was only enough space left in the gym for myself (out there all alone in the middle). Such an honor to be a part of that group!

Well, if that wasn't enough, I had some fine pre-teens who learned to use those big Sesame Street type puppets and they put on some puppet shows for the people in the nursing home and the church. Such fun!

In between all this, my granddaughter, Stephie, decided to get here and I had to fly via a small airline to Lansing to be with my daughter. It was a terrific flight—the stewardesses stood at the front of the plane and tossed Twinkies to all the passengers and we had a ball! Of course, Stephie was a winner and her parents were ecstatic! And her "Nana" was NUTS! (She was our first grandbaby—couldn't you guess?)

When I returned home, we were in the middle of The Governor's Project Competition Program. One year, I was the chairman and the steering committee decided as a project to buy land for a park and furnish it. So, to raise money, we decided to have the "World's Wildest Yard Sale" and we had loads of people participating, making it a grand success! We gave away a riding lawnmower, a yard (lots of grass), a pig (donated by a local cancer doctor); had wheelbarrow races, sold yardsticks ($1.00) and had a yard sale and various food vendors. WE GOT THE PARK! HEDGES!

(MY "PROFESSIONAL" EXPERIENCE WHILE IN WAVERLY HALL. Not much pay No respect, lots of gas, and too much work! BUT FUN!)

- ✓ I worked for two years with Hughston Clinic. I first worked in the steno pool until the new Hughston Clinic was finished. I was then promoted to Dr. Hughston's (AKA Dr. Knee) office as his secretary.
- ✓ Worked at home for a group of court stenographers.
- ✓ Corporate Secretary for the Waverly Hall Telephone Company.
- ✓ Went into the Bread business at my home! I purchased the wheat from Arrowhead, ground it into flour and made a wide variety of breads and rolls and various sweet creations, which were sold through the Farm House in Ellerslie, GA. A very successful venture!

After selling the house to move for my husband's work, the woman who purchased it had it demolished. What a shame! I am sure many of the family members had ill feelings about that.

At that time, Ollie received a promotion to terminal manager in Augusta Georgia, where we agreed to stay for a year and then move into the job of Safety Director of the Corporation (in Pennsylvania). Old Ollie really did a good job, making over a million that year and all of a sudden, the Safety Director's job went out the window, and so did Ollie. (Seems his year there in Augusta was so good they wanted him to stay!) He retired.

We bought a cabin at the top of Georgia, in Blue Ridge, and he just said, "I'm through!" (He had learned a lot, getting the AA degree.) AN ADDENDUM TO OUR 62 YEARS, THOUGH I'M SURE YOU DON'T REALLY NEED IT!

I just wanted to mention that for ten years after my mother-in-law died, we traveled in our motor home, working as "Work Campers" and had a wonderful time meeting all kinds of people and seeing things such as the Southern Bighorns, where we took care of three campgrounds, Detroit Lakes Campgrounds, Golf Course (Ollie built a new golf course, there and I taught "Computers for Dummies" and Arthritic water exercises and was a general hostess.) We also wintered in Texas and in New York state, while waiting for other jobs. Ollie also served at Diamond Lure Campground as resident speaker at the services in Fern Gully, there; providing all the jobs a preacher would. He was even fortunate enough to baptize a man; what a distinct pleasure that was.

We have pictures we made of our congregation – 25 beautiful people!

(Oh yes, I forgot; our friend asked him to officiate at his wife's funeral, and he was happy to say, "Yes." He really had a lot of friends.)

Author's Note

THANKS FOR READING ALL ABOUT HIM AND HIS WONDERFUL BLESSINGS ON OUR LIFE. WE ARE SO THANKFUL FOR HIS PATIENCE WITH US AND FOR THE OPPORTUNITY TO TELL OTHERS THIS TRUE STORY ABOUT HIS HEDGES AND LOVE!

OUR PERSONAL THANKS TO THOSE FRIENDS WHO ENCOURAGED US THROUGH THEIR LOVE AND FAITHFUL ASSISTANCE IN MAKING THIS BOOK A REALITY FOR THE LORD'S SAKE!

My husband (and collaborator) (Ollie/Marshall)
My friends and relatives for editing this book, and loving me so much.
Rev. Don Wilhite, my mother's dear pastor (for his encouragement & Prayer)
Brother Norman Drummond (A Chaplain at Calvary Gardens
Columbus, GA) for sending us to you my publisher.

Printed in the United States
By Bookmasters